50 Watermelon Recipes for Home

By: Kelly Johnson

Table of Contents

- Watermelon Pita Bread Pizza
- Watermelon Smoothie Pops
- Watermelon and Mango Salad
- Watermelon and Cucumber Agua Fresca
- Watermelon and Tomato Salad
- Watermelon Ice Cubes
- Watermelon and Jalapeño Salsa
- Watermelon Chicken Skewers
- Watermelon Frozen Yogurt
- Watermelon and Spinach Salad
- Watermelon and Grapefruit Juice
- Watermelon Rice Pudding
- Watermelon Muffins
- Watermelon and Cilantro Salsa
- Watermelon Breakfast Bowl
- Watermelon and Peach Salad

Watermelon Salad

Ingredients:

- 4 cups watermelon, cubed
- 1/2 cup feta cheese, crumbled
- 1/4 cup red onion, thinly sliced
- 1/4 cup fresh mint, chopped
- 2 tablespoons olive oil
- 1 tablespoon balsamic vinegar
- Salt and pepper to taste

Instructions:

1. In a large bowl, combine watermelon, feta cheese, red onion, and mint.
2. Drizzle with olive oil and balsamic vinegar.
3. Season with salt and pepper.
4. Gently toss to combine and serve chilled.

Watermelon Smoothie

Ingredients:

- 2 cups watermelon, cubed and frozen
- 1 banana
- 1/2 cup Greek yogurt
- 1/2 cup coconut water
- 1 tablespoon honey (optional)

Instructions:

1. Blend all ingredients in a blender until smooth.
2. Adjust sweetness with honey if needed.
3. Pour into glasses and serve immediately.

Watermelon Gazpacho

Ingredients:

- 4 cups watermelon, cubed
- 1 cucumber, peeled and diced
- 1 red bell pepper, diced
- 1 small red onion, diced
- 2 tablespoons lime juice
- 2 tablespoons olive oil
- Salt and pepper to taste

Instructions:

1. In a blender, combine watermelon, cucumber, red bell pepper, and red onion.
2. Blend until smooth.
3. Stir in lime juice and olive oil.
4. Season with salt and pepper.
5. Chill before serving.

Watermelon Feta Salad

Ingredients:

- 4 cups watermelon, cubed
- 1 cup feta cheese, crumbled
- 1/4 cup red onion, thinly sliced
- 1/4 cup fresh basil, chopped
- 2 tablespoons olive oil
- 1 tablespoon red wine vinegar
- Salt and pepper to taste

Instructions:

1. In a large bowl, combine watermelon, feta cheese, red onion, and basil.
2. Drizzle with olive oil and red wine vinegar.
3. Season with salt and pepper.
4. Toss gently and serve.

Watermelon Popsicles

Ingredients:

- 4 cups watermelon, cubed
- 1/4 cup lime juice
- 2 tablespoons honey

Instructions:

1. Blend watermelon, lime juice, and honey until smooth.
2. Pour mixture into popsicle molds.
3. Insert sticks and freeze until solid (about 4-6 hours).

Watermelon Sorbet

Ingredients:

- 4 cups watermelon, cubed
- 1/2 cup sugar
- 1/4 cup lime juice

Instructions:

1. Blend watermelon until smooth.
2. Stir in sugar and lime juice.
3. Pour mixture into a shallow dish and freeze, stirring every 30 minutes until firm.

Watermelon Juice

Ingredients:

- 4 cups watermelon, cubed
- 1 tablespoon lime juice
- 1 tablespoon honey (optional)

Instructions:

1. Blend watermelon until smooth.
2. Strain through a fine-mesh sieve if desired.
3. Stir in lime juice and honey if using.
4. Chill before serving.

Enjoy these refreshing watermelon recipes!

Watermelon Slush

Ingredients:

- 4 cups watermelon, cubed and frozen
- 1/2 cup lime juice
- 1/4 cup honey or agave syrup
- 1/2 cup water or coconut water

Instructions:

1. Blend frozen watermelon, lime juice, honey, and water until smooth.
2. Adjust sweetness to taste by adding more honey if needed.
3. Serve immediately or freeze for a firmer texture.

Watermelon Mint Cooler

Ingredients:

- 4 cups watermelon, cubed
- 1/4 cup fresh mint leaves
- 1/4 cup lime juice
- 2 tablespoons honey or sugar
- 1/2 cup sparkling water or soda

Instructions:

1. Blend watermelon, mint leaves, lime juice, and honey until smooth.
2. Strain mixture through a fine-mesh sieve into a pitcher.
3. Stir in sparkling water or soda.
4. Serve over ice.

Watermelon and Cucumber Salad

Ingredients:

- 4 cups watermelon, cubed
- 1 cucumber, peeled and diced
- 1/4 cup red onion, thinly sliced
- 1/4 cup fresh cilantro, chopped
- 2 tablespoons lime juice
- 1 tablespoon olive oil
- Salt and pepper to taste

Instructions:

1. In a large bowl, combine watermelon, cucumber, red onion, and cilantro.
2. Drizzle with lime juice and olive oil.
3. Season with salt and pepper.
4. Toss gently and serve chilled.

Watermelon Salsa

Ingredients:

- 3 cups watermelon, diced
- 1/2 cup red bell pepper, diced
- 1/4 cup red onion, finely chopped
- 1 jalapeño, seeded and minced
- 2 tablespoons lime juice
- 1/4 cup fresh cilantro, chopped
- Salt to taste

Instructions:

1. Combine watermelon, red bell pepper, red onion, and jalapeño in a bowl.
2. Stir in lime juice and cilantro.
3. Season with salt to taste.
4. Chill before serving.

Watermelon Gazpacho

Ingredients:

- 4 cups watermelon, cubed
- 1 cucumber, peeled and diced
- 1 red bell pepper, diced
- 1 small red onion, diced
- 2 tablespoons lime juice
- 2 tablespoons olive oil
- Salt and pepper to taste

Instructions:

1. In a blender, combine watermelon, cucumber, red bell pepper, and red onion.
2. Blend until smooth.
3. Stir in lime juice and olive oil.
4. Season with salt and pepper.
5. Chill before serving.

Watermelon and Basil Salad

Ingredients:

- 4 cups watermelon, cubed
- 1/4 cup fresh basil leaves, torn
- 1/4 cup crumbled feta cheese (optional)
- 2 tablespoons balsamic vinegar
- 1 tablespoon olive oil
- Salt and pepper to taste

Instructions:

1. In a large bowl, combine watermelon and basil.
2. Drizzle with balsamic vinegar and olive oil.
3. Season with salt and pepper.
4. Toss gently and serve.

Enjoy these refreshing and vibrant watermelon recipes!

Watermelon Pizza

Ingredients:

- 1 large round watermelon slice (about 1 inch thick)
- 1/2 cup Greek yogurt
- 2 tablespoons honey or agave syrup
- 1/2 cup fresh berries (e.g., blueberries, raspberries)
- 1/4 cup sliced almonds or chopped nuts
- Fresh mint leaves for garnish

Instructions:

1. Place the watermelon slice on a serving platter.
2. Spread Greek yogurt evenly over the top.
3. Drizzle with honey or agave syrup.
4. Top with fresh berries and sliced almonds.
5. Garnish with fresh mint leaves.
6. Slice into wedges and serve immediately.

Watermelon and Arugula Salad

Ingredients:

- 4 cups watermelon, cubed
- 2 cups arugula
- 1/4 cup red onion, thinly sliced
- 1/4 cup crumbled goat cheese or feta cheese
- 2 tablespoons olive oil
- 1 tablespoon balsamic vinegar
- Salt and pepper to taste

Instructions:

1. In a large bowl, combine watermelon, arugula, red onion, and cheese.
2. Drizzle with olive oil and balsamic vinegar.
3. Season with salt and pepper.
4. Toss gently and serve chilled.

Watermelon Lemonade

Ingredients:

- 4 cups watermelon, cubed
- 1/2 cup fresh lemon juice
- 1/4 cup sugar or honey (adjust to taste)
- 2 cups cold water
- Ice cubes

Instructions:

1. Blend watermelon until smooth.
2. Strain through a fine-mesh sieve into a pitcher.
3. Stir in lemon juice, sugar, and cold water.
4. Mix until sugar is dissolved.
5. Serve over ice.

Watermelon Smoothie Bowl

Ingredients:

- 2 cups watermelon, frozen and cubed
- 1 banana
- 1/2 cup Greek yogurt
- 1/4 cup coconut water or milk
- Toppings: granola, fresh fruit, chia seeds, coconut flakes

Instructions:

1. Blend frozen watermelon, banana, Greek yogurt, and coconut water until smooth.
2. Pour into a bowl and add your favorite toppings.
3. Serve immediately.

Watermelon and Strawberry Salad

Ingredients:

- 3 cups watermelon, cubed
- 1 cup strawberries, sliced
- 1/4 cup fresh basil or mint, chopped
- 2 tablespoons lime juice
- 1 tablespoon honey or agave syrup

Instructions:

1. In a large bowl, combine watermelon, strawberries, and herbs.
2. Drizzle with lime juice and honey.
3. Toss gently and serve.

Watermelon Chia Pudding

Ingredients:

- 2 cups watermelon, pureed
- 1/2 cup chia seeds
- 1 cup almond milk or other plant-based milk
- 2 tablespoons honey or maple syrup

Instructions:

1. In a bowl, mix chia seeds, almond milk, and honey.
2. Let sit for about 30 minutes, stirring occasionally.
3. Stir in watermelon puree.
4. Refrigerate for at least 2 hours or overnight until thickened.

Watermelon and Shrimp Ceviche

Ingredients:

- 2 cups watermelon, cubed
- 1/2 pound cooked shrimp, chopped
- 1/4 cup red onion, finely chopped
- 1 jalapeño, seeded and minced
- 2 tablespoons lime juice
- 1/4 cup fresh cilantro, chopped
- Salt and pepper to taste

Instructions:

1. In a bowl, combine watermelon, shrimp, red onion, and jalapeño.
2. Stir in lime juice and cilantro.
3. Season with salt and pepper.
4. Chill before serving.

Enjoy these refreshing and flavorful watermelon recipes!

Watermelon and Blueberry Salad

Ingredients:

- 4 cups watermelon, cubed
- 1 cup blueberries
- 1/4 cup fresh mint leaves, chopped
- 1/4 cup feta cheese, crumbled (optional)
- 2 tablespoons honey or agave syrup
- 1 tablespoon lime juice

Instructions:

1. In a large bowl, combine watermelon, blueberries, and mint leaves.
2. If using, sprinkle with crumbled feta cheese.
3. Drizzle with honey and lime juice.
4. Toss gently and serve chilled.

Watermelon and Prosciutto Skewers

Ingredients:

- 2 cups watermelon, cubed
- 6 slices prosciutto, cut into thirds
- Fresh basil leaves
- Balsamic glaze for drizzling

Instructions:

1. Thread a piece of watermelon, a basil leaf, and a piece of prosciutto onto each skewer.
2. Arrange skewers on a serving platter.
3. Drizzle with balsamic glaze before serving.

Watermelon Ice Cream

Ingredients:

- 4 cups watermelon, cubed and pureed
- 1 cup heavy cream
- 1/2 cup sugar
- 1/2 cup milk
- 1 teaspoon vanilla extract

Instructions:

1. In a bowl, mix together watermelon puree, cream, sugar, milk, and vanilla extract.
2. Pour mixture into an ice cream maker and churn according to the manufacturer's instructions.
3. Transfer to a container and freeze until firm.

Watermelon and Avocado Salad

Ingredients:

- 4 cups watermelon, cubed
- 1 avocado, diced
- 1/4 cup red onion, finely chopped
- 1/4 cup fresh cilantro, chopped
- 2 tablespoons lime juice
- Salt and pepper to taste

Instructions:

1. In a large bowl, combine watermelon, avocado, red onion, and cilantro.
2. Drizzle with lime juice.
3. Season with salt and pepper.
4. Toss gently and serve immediately.

Watermelon Mojito

Ingredients:

- 2 cups watermelon, cubed
- 10 fresh mint leaves
- 2 tablespoons lime juice
- 2 tablespoons sugar or simple syrup
- 1/2 cup white rum (optional)
- Sparkling water
- Ice cubes

Instructions:

1. Muddle mint leaves and sugar in a glass.
2. Add watermelon cubes and lime juice. Muddle again.
3. Fill the glass with ice and add rum if using.
4. Top with sparkling water and stir.
5. Garnish with additional mint leaves and watermelon slices.

Watermelon Cupcakes

Ingredients:

- 1 1/2 cups all-purpose flour
- 1 cup sugar
- 1/2 teaspoon baking powder
- 1/4 teaspoon baking soda
- 1/4 teaspoon salt
- 1/2 cup unsalted butter, softened
- 1/2 cup watermelon puree
- 2 large eggs
- 1/2 teaspoon vanilla extract
- 1/4 cup milk

Instructions:

1. Preheat oven to 350°F (175°C) and line a muffin tin with cupcake liners.
2. In a bowl, whisk together flour, sugar, baking powder, baking soda, and salt.
3. In another bowl, beat butter until creamy. Add watermelon puree, eggs, and vanilla extract.
4. Gradually mix in the dry ingredients, alternating with milk.
5. Divide batter among cupcake liners and bake for 18-20 minutes or until a toothpick comes out clean.
6. Let cool before frosting.

Watermelon Granita

Ingredients:

- 4 cups watermelon, cubed and pureed
- 1/2 cup sugar
- 1/4 cup lemon juice

Instructions:

1. In a bowl, mix watermelon puree, sugar, and lemon juice.
2. Pour mixture into a shallow dish and freeze.
3. Every 30 minutes, scrape the mixture with a fork to create a fluffy texture.
4. Continue until granita is fully frozen and fluffy.

Enjoy these delightful watermelon recipes!

Watermelon and Pineapple Salad

Ingredients:

- 3 cups watermelon, cubed
- 2 cups pineapple, cubed
- 1/4 cup red onion, thinly sliced
- 1/4 cup fresh mint or basil, chopped
- 2 tablespoons lime juice
- 1 tablespoon honey or agave syrup (optional)
- Salt and pepper to taste

Instructions:

1. In a large bowl, combine watermelon, pineapple, and red onion.
2. Drizzle with lime juice and honey if using.
3. Add fresh mint or basil.
4. Season with salt and pepper.
5. Toss gently and serve chilled.

Watermelon BBQ Ribs

Ingredients:

- 2 lbs pork ribs
- 2 cups watermelon juice
- 1 cup BBQ sauce
- 1/4 cup apple cider vinegar
- 2 tablespoons honey
- 2 cloves garlic, minced
- 1 teaspoon smoked paprika
- Salt and pepper to taste

Instructions:

1. Preheat oven to 300°F (150°C).
2. Season ribs with salt and pepper.
3. In a bowl, mix watermelon juice, BBQ sauce, apple cider vinegar, honey, garlic, and smoked paprika.
4. Place ribs in a baking dish and cover with the sauce mixture.
5. Cover with foil and bake for 2.5-3 hours.
6. Remove foil and broil for 5-10 minutes to caramelize the sauce.

Watermelon Lime Sorbet

Ingredients:

- 4 cups watermelon, cubed
- 1/2 cup sugar
- 1/4 cup lime juice
- 1/2 cup water

Instructions:

1. Blend watermelon until smooth.
2. Stir in sugar, lime juice, and water.
3. Pour mixture into a shallow dish and freeze.
4. Every 30 minutes, scrape the mixture with a fork to create a fluffy texture.
5. Continue until sorbet is fully frozen and fluffy.

Watermelon and Cucumber Gazpacho

Ingredients:

- 3 cups watermelon, cubed
- 1 cucumber, peeled and diced
- 1/2 cup red bell pepper, diced
- 1/4 cup red onion, diced
- 2 tablespoons lime juice
- 2 tablespoons olive oil
- Salt and pepper to taste

Instructions:

1. In a blender, combine watermelon, cucumber, red bell pepper, and red onion.
2. Blend until smooth.
3. Stir in lime juice and olive oil.
4. Season with salt and pepper.
5. Chill before serving.

Watermelon and Goat Cheese Salad

Ingredients:

- 4 cups watermelon, cubed
- 1/2 cup goat cheese, crumbled
- 1/4 cup red onion, thinly sliced
- 1/4 cup fresh basil or mint, chopped
- 2 tablespoons balsamic glaze
- Salt and pepper to taste

Instructions:

1. In a large bowl, combine watermelon, goat cheese, and red onion.
2. Drizzle with balsamic glaze.
3. Garnish with fresh basil or mint.
4. Season with salt and pepper.
5. Toss gently and serve.

Watermelon Jelly

Ingredients:

- 4 cups watermelon juice
- 1/2 cup sugar
- 1/4 cup lemon juice
- 1/4 cup water
- 1 packet (1/4 oz) unflavored gelatin

Instructions:

1. In a small bowl, dissolve gelatin in water and let sit for 5 minutes.
2. Heat watermelon juice in a saucepan and stir in sugar until dissolved.
3. Remove from heat and stir in gelatin mixture until fully dissolved.
4. Stir in lemon juice.
5. Pour into molds or a dish and refrigerate until set (about 4 hours).

Watermelon Infused Vodka

Ingredients:

- 4 cups watermelon, cubed
- 1 bottle (750 ml) vodka

Instructions:

1. Place watermelon cubes in a large jar or pitcher.
2. Pour vodka over the watermelon.
3. Seal and refrigerate for 3-5 days, shaking occasionally.
4. Strain out watermelon and transfer vodka to a clean bottle.
5. Serve chilled or use in cocktails.

Enjoy these creative and refreshing watermelon recipes!

Watermelon Pita Bread Pizza

Ingredients:

- 2 large pita breads
- 1 cup Greek yogurt
- 1 tablespoon honey
- 1 cup watermelon, cubed
- 1/4 cup fresh basil, chopped
- 1/4 cup crumbled feta cheese (optional)
- 1 tablespoon balsamic glaze (optional)

Instructions:

1. Preheat oven to 400°F (200°C).
2. Place pita breads on a baking sheet.
3. Mix Greek yogurt and honey, then spread over the pita breads.
4. Top with watermelon cubes and sprinkle with basil and feta cheese if using.
5. Bake for 5-7 minutes, until the pita is crispy.
6. Drizzle with balsamic glaze before serving.

Watermelon Smoothie Pops

Ingredients:

- 4 cups watermelon, cubed and frozen
- 1/2 cup Greek yogurt
- 2 tablespoons honey or agave syrup
- 1/4 cup lime juice

Instructions:

1. Blend frozen watermelon, Greek yogurt, honey, and lime juice until smooth.
2. Pour mixture into popsicle molds.
3. Insert sticks and freeze until solid (about 4-6 hours).

Watermelon and Mango Salad

Ingredients:

- 3 cups watermelon, cubed
- 2 cups mango, cubed
- 1/4 cup red onion, thinly sliced
- 1/4 cup fresh mint or cilantro, chopped
- 2 tablespoons lime juice
- 1 tablespoon honey (optional)
- Salt to taste

Instructions:

1. In a large bowl, combine watermelon, mango, and red onion.
2. Drizzle with lime juice and honey if using.
3. Add mint or cilantro.
4. Season with salt and toss gently.
5. Serve chilled.

Watermelon and Cucumber Agua Fresca

Ingredients:

- 4 cups watermelon, cubed
- 1 cucumber, peeled and chopped
- 1/4 cup lime juice
- 2 tablespoons sugar or honey
- 2 cups cold water

Instructions:

1. Blend watermelon, cucumber, lime juice, and sugar until smooth.
2. Strain through a fine-mesh sieve into a pitcher.
3. Stir in cold water.
4. Chill before serving over ice.

Watermelon and Tomato Salad

Ingredients:

- 3 cups watermelon, cubed
- 2 cups cherry tomatoes, halved
- 1/4 cup red onion, thinly sliced
- 1/4 cup fresh basil, chopped
- 2 tablespoons olive oil
- 1 tablespoon balsamic vinegar
- Salt and pepper to taste

Instructions:

1. In a large bowl, combine watermelon, cherry tomatoes, and red onion.
2. Drizzle with olive oil and balsamic vinegar.
3. Add fresh basil.
4. Season with salt and pepper.
5. Toss gently and serve.

Watermelon Ice Cubes

Ingredients:

- 2 cups watermelon, cubed
- 1/4 cup lime juice
- Fresh mint leaves (optional)

Instructions:

1. Blend watermelon until smooth.
2. Stir in lime juice.
3. Pour mixture into ice cube trays.
4. Add mint leaves if desired.
5. Freeze until solid.

Watermelon and Jalapeño Salsa

Ingredients:

- 3 cups watermelon, diced
- 1 jalapeño, seeded and minced
- 1/4 cup red onion, finely chopped
- 1/4 cup cilantro, chopped
- 2 tablespoons lime juice
- Salt to taste

Instructions:

1. In a bowl, combine watermelon, jalapeño, red onion, and cilantro.
2. Stir in lime juice.
3. Season with salt to taste.
4. Chill before serving.

Enjoy these refreshing and unique watermelon recipes!

Watermelon Chicken Skewers

Ingredients:

- 2 cups watermelon, cubed
- 1 lb chicken breast, cut into bite-sized pieces
- 1/4 cup soy sauce
- 2 tablespoons honey
- 2 tablespoons olive oil
- 2 cloves garlic, minced
- 1 tablespoon fresh ginger, minced
- Salt and pepper to taste
- Wooden skewers, soaked in water

Instructions:

1. In a bowl, mix soy sauce, honey, olive oil, garlic, and ginger.
2. Add chicken pieces and marinate for at least 30 minutes.
3. Preheat grill or grill pan to medium-high heat.
4. Thread chicken and watermelon cubes onto skewers, alternating between the two.
5. Grill skewers for 3-4 minutes on each side, until chicken is cooked through and watermelon is slightly caramelized.
6. Season with salt and pepper before serving.

Watermelon Frozen Yogurt

Ingredients:

- 4 cups watermelon, cubed and frozen
- 1 cup Greek yogurt
- 1/4 cup honey or agave syrup
- 1 tablespoon lime juice

Instructions:

1. Blend frozen watermelon, Greek yogurt, honey, and lime juice until smooth.
2. Pour mixture into a freezer-safe container.
3. Freeze for at least 2 hours, stirring occasionally to prevent ice crystals.
4. Scoop and serve.

Watermelon and Spinach Salad

Ingredients:

- 4 cups watermelon, cubed
- 2 cups fresh spinach leaves
- 1/4 cup red onion, thinly sliced
- 1/4 cup crumbled goat cheese or feta cheese
- 2 tablespoons balsamic vinegar
- 1 tablespoon olive oil
- Salt and pepper to taste

Instructions:

1. In a large bowl, combine watermelon, spinach, and red onion.
2. Drizzle with balsamic vinegar and olive oil.
3. Sprinkle with goat cheese or feta cheese.
4. Season with salt and pepper.
5. Toss gently and serve.

Watermelon and Grapefruit Juice

Ingredients:

- 3 cups watermelon, cubed
- 1 cup grapefruit juice (freshly squeezed or store-bought)
- 1 tablespoon honey or agave syrup (optional)
- Ice cubes

Instructions:

1. Blend watermelon until smooth.
2. Strain through a fine-mesh sieve into a pitcher.
3. Stir in grapefruit juice and honey if using.
4. Chill before serving over ice.

Watermelon Rice Pudding

Ingredients:

- 1 cup cooked rice
- 2 cups watermelon puree
- 1 cup milk (any kind)
- 1/4 cup sugar or honey
- 1 teaspoon vanilla extract
- Fresh mint for garnish (optional)

Instructions:

1. In a saucepan, combine watermelon puree, milk, and sugar or honey. Heat over medium heat until warm.
2. Stir in cooked rice and cook for 5-7 minutes, until the mixture thickens slightly.
3. Remove from heat and stir in vanilla extract.
4. Let cool and serve warm or chilled, garnished with fresh mint if desired.

Watermelon Muffins

Ingredients:

- 1 1/2 cups all-purpose flour
- 1 cup sugar
- 1/2 teaspoon baking powder
- 1/2 teaspoon baking soda
- 1/4 teaspoon salt
- 1/2 cup unsalted butter, melted
- 1 cup watermelon puree
- 1 large egg
- 1/2 teaspoon vanilla extract

Instructions:

1. Preheat oven to 350°F (175°C) and line a muffin tin with paper liners.
2. In a bowl, whisk together flour, sugar, baking powder, baking soda, and salt.
3. In another bowl, mix melted butter, watermelon puree, egg,

and vanilla extract. 4. Combine wet and dry ingredients, mixing just until combined. 5. Divide batter among muffin cups. 6. Bake for 18-20 minutes, or until a toothpick inserted into the center comes out clean. 7. Cool on a wire rack before serving.

Enjoy these diverse and delicious watermelon recipes!

Watermelon and Cilantro Salsa

Ingredients:

- 3 cups watermelon, diced
- 1/4 cup red onion, finely chopped
- 1 jalapeño, seeded and minced
- 1/4 cup fresh cilantro, chopped
- 2 tablespoons lime juice
- Salt and pepper to taste

Instructions:

1. In a bowl, combine watermelon, red onion, jalapeño, and cilantro.
2. Drizzle with lime juice and season with salt and pepper.
3. Toss gently to mix.
4. Serve immediately or chill for 30 minutes to allow flavors to meld.

Watermelon Breakfast Bowl

Ingredients:

- 2 cups watermelon, cubed
- 1/2 cup Greek yogurt
- 1/4 cup granola
- 1 tablespoon honey or maple syrup
- Fresh berries (e.g., blueberries, strawberries) for topping
- Fresh mint leaves for garnish (optional)

Instructions:

1. In a bowl, arrange watermelon cubes as the base.
2. Top with Greek yogurt and granola.
3. Drizzle with honey or maple syrup.
4. Add fresh berries and garnish with mint leaves if desired.
5. Serve immediately.

Watermelon and Peach Salad

Ingredients:

- 3 cups watermelon, cubed
- 2 peaches, sliced
- 1/4 cup red onion, thinly sliced
- 1/4 cup fresh basil or mint, chopped
- 2 tablespoons lime juice
- 1 tablespoon olive oil
- Salt and pepper to taste

Instructions:

1. In a large bowl, combine watermelon, peaches, and red onion.
2. Drizzle with lime juice and olive oil.
3. Add fresh basil or mint.
4. Season with salt and pepper.
5. Toss gently and serve chilled.

Enjoy these refreshing and vibrant recipes!

9 798330 428502